There Are Too Many Words In My House - Bruce Weber

- A Single Volume.
- First Edition.
- 120 pages.
- Trade Paperback.
- American contemporary poetry collection by a single author.

Rogue Scholars Press
http://www.roguescholars.com

Author Contact Information:

Bruce Weber
635 Manorville Road
Saugerties, NY 12477

Design and layout by C. D. Johnson

Cover and frontispiece artwork, "Constellation", Copyright by Joanne Pagano Weber

Interior artwork, "Interior 1", "Interior 4", "Interior 7", "Interior 12", Copyright by Arturo Rodriguez

ISBN-13: 978-1-942463-03-0
ISBN-10: 1-942463-03-0

Published by Rogue Scholars Press
New York, NY - USA

THERE ARE TOO MANY WORDS IN MY HOUSE

Bruce Weber

Published by Rogue Scholars Press
http://www.roguescholars.com

To My Mother Sylvia
(1917-2013)

Table Of Contents

Table Of Contents

CONVALESCENCE

INTERIORS

Bruce Weber is the author of five previously published books of poetry: *"These Poems are Not Pretty"* (Miami: Palmetto Press, 1992), *"How the Poem Died"* (New York: Linear Arts, 1998), *"Poetic Justice"* (New York: Ikon Press, 2004), *"The First Time I Had Sex with T. S. Eliot"* (New York: Venom Press, 2004), and *"The Break-up of My First Marriage"* (Rogue Scholars Press, 2009).

Bruce's work has appeared in numerous magazines, as well as in several anthologies, including *"Up is Up, But So Is Down: Downtown Writings, 1978-1992"* (New York: New York University, 2006), *"Riverine: An Anthology of Hudson Valley Writers"* (New Paltz, New York: Codhill Press, 2007), and *"The Unbearables Big Book of Sex"* (Autonomedia, 2010). He has performed regularly in the Tri-State area, both alone and for many years with his former performance group, **Bruce Weber's No Chance Ensemble**, which produced the CD, *"Let's Dine Like Jack Johnson Tonight"* (http://members.aol/com/ncensemble).

For twenty-five years, Bruce produced the **Alternative New Year's Day Spoken Word / Performance Extravaganza** in New York City, and next year he will organize a marathon event featuring writers, performance artists and musicians on New Year's Day in Kingston, New York. He moved with his wife, the artist and writer Joanne Pagano Weber, to Saugerties in 2018.

A former museum curator and director of research and exhibitions for a major gallery in New York, he has organized many exhibitions and authored numerous publications on American art. Currently Bruce is lecturing, writing and curating exhibitions revolving around the historic Woodstock art colony.

–

Some of these poems have appeared in *A Gathering of the Tribes*, *Home Planet News*, *Before the Dawn*, *Pa'lante a la Luz (Charge into the Light)*, *Green Kill*, *Art Times Journal*, *Chronogram*, *Brownstone Poets Anthology*, *Great Weather for MEDIA*, *South Florida Poetry Journal*, and *Like Light: 25 Years of Poetry and Prose by Bright Hill Poets & Writers*, among others.

The poems in **There Are Too Many Words in My House** are magnificent illustrations of a poet who has fine-tuned his craft and honed his artistry. Bruce Weber has always been a poet of exploration, boundary breaking and unbridled heart and spirit. I know this because I've known him for more than 30 years.

Years ago he read a poem at a book store in Miami: "Brick Brick Brick Brick Brick Brick Brick Brick Brick Brick"... for the entire page. And then he sat down. It blew me away. Not because he invented the idea that one word repeated again and again could be considered a poem, (I don't think he did) but because he dared to be Brick at a time when the rest of us were Glass. He has always thrown stones at convention. He has always poked the bear.

I love how Weber's poems go sideways when I least expect it. Like great jazz riffs, his lines go off in a sequence of metaphors or images. Sometimes they come back, sometimes they don't:

> these strange beautiful creatures tantalized her imagination.
> made her swing through the air like a cowboy's lasso. exchanged
> her vocabulary of rocks and snails and paper dolls for aeronautic
> words like wind thrust or avalanche till she was turned inside out
> with confusion about wind and the islands of sanctuary in her
> rear view mirror and the path through the tall cedar grove lined
> with stones awaiting the accidental slip of a shoe...

*(From **"The Woods Beside the House"**)*

Ginsberg famously walked with Whitman. Weber walks with Breton and Cézanne:

> *The wine bottle is filled against the sky*
> *and the off-beat rules of Cézanne.*
>
> *The impossible is capricious*
> *and the capricious is impossible.*
>
> *The single bicycle wheel turns*
> *and the world is going Dada.*

*(From **"Poem for Cézanne"**)*

Going Dada indeed. Weber has spent his life in museums and art galleries. He has had a long career as art historian and curator. He knows his way around canvasses, pigments, brushstrokes and perspective. I can't help think his expertise in that world has informed his imagination and choices in this one—the world of language and poetry.

In addition, Weber's poetics might also be inherited in an imaginative sense:

> *my grandpa would stand at the cliff of things/*
> *anticipating long leaps / jumps into catastrophes /*
> *last looks into the molten core of the world /*
> demanding brevity / a ruthless red penciller /
> of romantic flights of fancy and gushing streams
> *of exuberance / this is why i'm a poet /…*

(From "Short Things")

Leaps and jumps have long been the syntax of Weber's language. But the adage, "Leap and the net will appear" does not apply to his poetry. These poems are not safe. They're radioactive. They glow in the dark. They linger in me like technetium, *"The Element That Can Make Bones Glow",* (BBC news reporter Laurence Knight, *BBC News Magazine*, May 30, 2015).

Perhaps there *are* too many words in Weber's house, but he knows which ones to single out, pluck them from mercurial walls, wrestle them onto the page and make them obey his outrageously brilliant broken rules. These poems slap me in the face, kick me in the balls, spit in my mouth, and hug me like I've been away too long. It's like I've come home, except someone put the doors on the ceiling.

— Lenny DellaRocca

FINDINGS

These have been impossible seasons
He said
Lighting a match
On the side of the barn
Then watching it flitter in the wind and go out.

These impossible seasons
Have tied up your mother's mind in sailor's knots
Have scurried for shelter in god's humble house
Have delivered bread when death stood by the door.

These have been impossible seasons
He said
Fingering through memories of his daughter's smile
The moment she surrendered to father time
Her face covered with grandmother's blue handkerchief.

Someday everything will be clear as old man Sumner's pond
And truth will tickle us under the arms
He said
Biting into a crab apple and spitting it out
Slamming a fist against the stomach of a mighty oak.

These have been impossible seasons
He said
Twisting a stick in the earth
Laughing as loud as a torrent of hail
Tapping the length of tobacco and paper
Against the barn door for luck.

When She Looked East

when she looked east the sky shattered / little glass chips
flying everywhere / it was a reminder of the war years /
the constant bombardment from the west / the roofs ablaze /
water spouting out of unfathomable places. after the war
she'd sit for days staring into the void or pretend to be
biting off the spring on a hand grenade. she'd count to
a thousand then move one small step at a time like she
was a rock prodded by a butterfly. she'd swallow a spoon
of porridge at the all night shelter and remember that
bright night of explosions falling like lightning and
thunder over and over in her dreams. she never was safe
from them / they chased her everywhere / she couldn't
get away / would never get away. it was something lost
in clouds. / blurry / out of focus / beyond the ken of normal
eyesight / doubled / twisted in the wind / damned / twisted
in the wind / she was doomed to the parade of bad echoes
of a long ago war ricocheting everywhere.

Findings

in
the
grip
of
the
spider
in the toehold of god
in the sightlines of serendipity
in the pursuit of sincerity
in the hasty chase after the blues
in the lucky range of your eyes
in the red hush of mars
in the beeping opinion of the creeky car
in the suddenly yelping throat of the dog
in the puzzling amorphousness of a puddle
in the great black umbrella that spits rain
in the assumption that breathes in deeply
in the conversation amidst stragglers and worms
i offer you a sniff and a cough
a bite and a kiss
a tremendous assumption
that leaps canyons
in all this
i will find you
yes i will find you
i
will
find
you

The Lament Of The Rain

the cats look on from their cozy perch / pleased to be laying
in the light of the sun pouring through the windows after days
of relentless rain / drowning the fields / submerging bridges /
playing a heartless song with the late autumn crops / toying
with love like an unbreakable knot / raising the ire on father
time and his merciless pledge to the clockmakers and time
keepers / while love swirls around them like a vortex / breaking
branches / casting off twigs / lambasting the liars and the
temperamental fiddlers strumming in a disingenuous measure
sure to gain the wrath of true romantics / and the young perfectly
suited couples wheeling baby carriages / the wind raising
the hackles on the backs of drifters sidestepping mudslides
left in the residue of the inconsolable rain / the cats rambling
to the floor / hissing and scratching / there's a hurricane flooding
the house but they're running around like children in the school
yard / fussing and carrying on / as shackles slip from hands /
as keys twist in old broken locks

The Egyptian Ring

that's such a nice eqyptian ring.
did you win it in a raffle?
did you pull it out of the sea?
did you inherit it from your grandmother?
i want to learn the mysteries of that ring
the enigmas of that ring
the long and short of that ring.
can you spell it out for me in hieroglyphics?
can you tie your past directly to the great pharaohs?
can you reveal your genetic link to the sun god ra?
please tell me about your place in the life and death cycle of ancient egypt;
the root your blood has traveled back to the tigrus and euphrates.
show me the secret hiding places of that ring.
the button to push to discover the dark past of that ring.
the foggy destiny of that ring;
predicting apocalypse
predicting the rising and setting of jupiter's moons
predicting everything becoming dust -- becoming ruin.
till all things fall.
till all things rise again.
till the cycle comes around once more.
that's such a nice egyptian ring

Callous Numbers

For Jack Tricarico

How did I not notice you standing in the rain
I wanted to apologize for loving you
It was a stone thrown through a wall
A daring point of juncture
Divided by twigs
And callous numbers
I wanted to jump
But you said "Eat first"
Those were long days
Among the mushrooms and birds
When they told me you jumped
I wet my pants
Some things are predictable
But not much
Especially among poodles and grande dames
Someday I will recognize you in a blur
A sign that expands in memory
But mostly sits there drooling
I'm an optimist
And these shoes are too tight
Arrange yourself across this lumpy old bed
Admire yourself in this long mirror
When day ebbs I'll telephone you collect
It's sudden these pangs
They burst in my gut
Like the 4th of july
I won't ever apologize again
These things hurdle across the city
Like bruised tiger cubs
Parched and itchy
After midnight arrives I'll buy you a new bicycle
And the air will get as thick as the morning porridge
We'll dance in the rain and the fog
Imagining simpler times
When the guy down the block
Introduced us to Don Perignon
And we celebrated every hour
Like Independence Day

Reminiscences

The early morning light reminds me of you.
The strange opinions.
The tangled hair.
The impossible odds.
Those were long days
Roped in bliss and tears.
Days that tugged at our collars
And slammed us against life
Like bumper cars.
I remember your voice
Rising above the din.
The echoe of expectations
Floating across the periphery
Of the world with a hiss.
The way time opened its hands
With a full alibi and a crush of sand.
We watched it pour into our lives like thunder.
We watched it twist in the wind like a tornado.
We watched it depart without any glances back or a tip of a cap.
Now memories linger on my doorstep marked with paint and words.
Now memories shout out with chalk across barren streets demanding a voice.
Now memories collide with stone and ash and time.
And I watch as the ghost of your memory passes into the fire.
Going going gone.

Something Was Razorbladed Out Of The Photo

something was razorbladed out of the photo, like squadrons of dark uniformed soldiers of a passing civilization, like garbage thrown in the narrow neck between tenements, like death on a high wire among dealers who want to cheat you, something was dyanamited to smithererens, without dignity, without regard for its elders, without respecting a higher calling, waving farewell to emma lazurus' promise, to walt whitman's energy in motion, to jacob riis' crusader spirit behind the camera, to magaret sanger's passion, to emma goldman's fiery speeches about the poor and forlorn, something has stripped away the soul of the city, the exchange every immigrant makes for a chance his children know a brighter future, something was disappearing in fog like a tug boat out in the harbor, beyond the eye of the paparazzi's camera, halfway down a flagpole, in the trash bins behind the metropolitan museum of art, in the community gardens nestled between cracks in the pavement.

Tilted Poem

the universe is tilted
he says
everything's falling a bit to the right
then a bit to the left
the world is tripping over its own feet
everything's slippery
unapproachable with a solid step
or an unimpeachable source
the wind roars
like an uncertain whale
rekindling the warmth
of another surer day
when i witnessed your apology in the mirror
now everything has turned blue
a redeemable blue
a reversible blue
a temptation of blue
in this poem
no one falls down
the road is paved with gold
you walk into my arms
carrying the weight of so many wars
the birds raise their horn to the sky
the universe
un
t
i
l
t
s
the movie camera is running
the lights go dim

The Bubble

the bubble broke
startling the federal bureau of investigation
quieting the loud rock band at izzy's emporium
spiriting off the drifters dreaming of shangri-la
in the distance the moon blushed
the crowd dispersed like sand falling from loose fingers
school children jumped through fiery hoops
the poor whimpering horde of hungry people
shuffled off like malfunctioning vacuum cleaners
after the day sunk into the sea
after the pizza man jumped on the subway track
after the stars in the sky fizzled into a cup as large as the milky way
i opened my repair kit
i nailed the bubble back together
i fixed the seams of the bubble like a masterful tailor
restoring the bubble to its rightful place in the universe
stories appeared in the press lauding my capable fingers
and my astonishing ability to heal the bubbles ailments
the bubble good as new
the bubble restored to all its glory
the bubble bouncing around like a happy infant

THE BLUE SIGNS

The Blue Signs

the signs have changed
they're now a startling blue
someone came at dawn
and exchanged the yellow for blue
i stumbled in front of the signs
while tying my shoes
it was a carefree stumble
i didn't worry where i landed
i was surrounded
by a wave of calm
that masqueraded as serenity
that drummed its fingers
along the protrusions in my scalp
it was comforting
to look at these signs
with their florid names
and simple patterns
they rang some exotic chime
in my imagination
these blue signs
circulated over my frame
like an avalanche of wonder
the sudden awakening of white letters
against a background of blue
that galloped like wild horses
across the panorama of blue
that lingered over the sidewalks
with a big contented smile of blue

A Strange Day

it was a strange day. tulips blossomed
as tall as midtown skyscrapers. denice
cried in a towel. the rock on the shelf
glowed mischievously. every bar room
leaned to the left. blue clouds walked
into the subway station and purred like
kittens. we wandered aimlessly through
tunnels looking for a silver lining.

it was a strange day. harvey raised a
drink and praised the sea and sky and
sun. he became consumed by the letter
s. tieing it around his throat like a scarf.
shamelessly plugging samantha's new
book. sandra's unhooked bra. susie's
invisible playmate. i stood in the sun
and waved at an airplane. i took out
my weasel and stared off to mars.
i rubbed the gleaming ball and promised
i would remain a virgin till man walked
on mars. all the s's in the universe
fell asleep and i was alone. finally,
gloriously. alone.

it was an aluminum day. a steel day. a
lead day. all the metal collectors were
happy. they jumped up like a mexican
bean dance. they galloped across the
city like a herd of happy horses. they
filled the lanes of the highways with
throbbing glee. they portrayed them —
selves as free of porcelain. bereft of
ivory. devoid of makeshift stainless
steel epiphanies.

it was a narrow day. a day difficult to
fit between sentences. a day thin as
forgetfulness. a day hiding under the
basement boiler. a day hibernating
in memory. a day split asunder. a day
disappearing down a manhole. a day
betraying sunlight. a day fizzling away
to nothing. a day like any other apocalypse.

Shush

there's a shush coming from the earth. this shush meanders through fields of cats meowing at the moon. it jumps over evergreen forests. it catapults sexy women on the covers of flirtatious magazines. it transcends every small morsel of morals caught up in a right wing conspiracy. throwing down its clothes. its gavel. its righteous call for freedom from noises interjecting themselves into the night. stirring the squirrels from high branches. moving across the muddy earth with a protest sign raised to the heavens. this shush sits in my berth protecting me from uncalled for fears. sprinkles cinnamon in my morning coffee. anticipates wrong from right with a twist of the head and a snap of the fingers. shushing away ramshackle sounds. overambitious anteaters. the adolescents raising the level of the music to the threshold of a supersonic jet. shusssssssssssssssssssssssssshhh.

What Is That Strange Humming?

what is that strange humming? is it a horde of mosquitoes circling its prey in the dark house across the way? is it the voice of a young girl oozing soap across the landscape of her skin? is it the refrigerator greeting a fresh gust of electricity seeping into its chilly bones? could it be coming from the hollow of the bark of that maple tree bending like a horse to drink from the pool of water along the road? could it be emanating from that halo on the head of st. sebastian in the scene of martyrdom from the period of the black plague? is it echoing in the memory of that old crone hobbling across the street to perch at the door of the cathedral with a cup and a plea? maybe its coming from behind the closed door of the maids in the attic or from the squirrels maneuvering acorns into the earth or maybe it's merely a shadow lingering in the full figure of an illusion or a preposterous trick played by an imposter lurking in the back roads of the mind holding a puppeteer's strings or maybe it's a void empty of sound bereft of hello's where all things dwindle to zero escaping into air like breath or electrons or the dust at the end of a long trail toward god and salvation and the cure for all things great and small.

Poem For Cézanne

The wine bottle is tilted against the sky
and the off-beat rules of Cézanne.

The impossible is capricious
and the capricious is impossible.

The single bicycle wheel turns
and the world is going Dada.

That was before beauty moved
into my house and stayed there.

The force of the sun's rays made me blush.
The stars in the sky exchanged looks.

Was I supposed to make love with her
under a blanket of suspicion?

The birds sometimes mate with bats.
They like their dark and heavy looks.

The birds chirp like nighthawks and
the bats whistle in three-part-harmony.

It's a respectable pursuit among the easily pleased
and the strong armed twisting life into impossible fruit.

Daring love to upset the apple cart of youth.
Bartering with truth's ability to ripen everything.

dear henrietta:

had a crazy dream last night. old man walton turned into trigger the horse and mrs. maple was transformed from a bed sore into a beautiful princess. its funny how dreams change rocks into streams or the delicate ballerina is launched like a rocket ship toward the outer galaxies in the quick wink of a sleepy eye. why i've had dreams where stone turns into quicksand and the abyss takes on the heroic character of abraham lincoln. where the implacable becomes solid as granite and the impossible throws away its crutches. if life was like dreams we'd maneuver out of desperate situations with a snap of our fingers. we'd sail off into the sunset and desire would carry us through every terrible rainstorm. we'd reverse the tragic consequences of ruptures in the water supply and i'd look you in the eye and tell you I love you without ever slipping and bruising my knee.

sincerely,

jacob

The Woodstock Poetry Festival

the poets come and go like seraphins. flitting into town on buses from as far away as dubuque or omaha. raising the spirits of townspeople like the world's a safer and more congenial place because of them. they get hoisted on the metaphorical shoulders of little boys and girls who want to grow up to be just like them. writing poems about the tail of comets / the hiss left behind by an unruly cat / or the juxtapositions of stars on a black-craypaper-sky in an elementary school production of peter pan. the poets come to town for the annual poetry festival and we fete them like royalty. worshipping them with applause. as if they're all wearing diadem's. their poems making this rickety old town stand up on its wobbly legs as solidly as the limestone church on the corner that's survived two hundred years of hail and brimstone. yes the poets come and go like seraphins. flitting into town on buses from as far away as dubuque or omaha.

Joy

i bring you joy.
pure unadulterated joy.
in a genie-shaped bottle.
in a vat as vast as the mohave desert.
in a football-sized field of fabulous phenomena.
this is my gift to the poor. to the rich. to the neglected middle.
accept it without qualms / trick handshakes / or double the money back offers.
gracefully. elegantly. luxuriously.
like a harvest of corn outstretching the far western horizon.
filling every pore of your soul like a waterfall.
like the infinite source of mountain spring water.
like the miraculous floating islands of lake titticatti.
permitting joy to bathe your senses.
without hesitation.
without requiring a telephone call to your parents.
without ever needing to look it up on google.
allowing joyfulness into your life
like a child's endless stream of sticky bubbles.
like a potpourri of keys opening impossible puzzles.

Sometimes I Want To

sometimes I want to tell you the story of the making of the universe. othertimes I want to scold you for being so swift on your feet. swifter than i who always apologizes to the speed of light. the astonishing things passing like ghosts in the night. shedding their husks and heavy overcoats. at these times the air is clear as a bottle of spring water. the mind moves in ridiculous places. counting time. breathing deeply in. convincing itself to stay out of the rain. the cold. the temperamental kitchen. it is at these times that the universe stands in proper posture. the wind runs through its hair but it does not blink. everything is as golden as apelles' apple. the universe spreads its wings and pulls us on its back and takes us on a flight among stars / comets / and blake's glimmering seraphin. it is at these times that all is well and the church bell rings. the church bell rings.

BETWEEN THE WARS

Short Things

i like to keep things short / minus heartache /
sweat / or theory / so things flow easily / gingerly /
without excess baggage or dirty looks from
strangers / i learned this at my grandpa's knee /
he was a curt man / without loose edges or moorings /
a tell it like it is man / habitual as clockwork /
without dangling strings or participles /
my grandpa would stand at the cliff of things /
anticipating long leaps / jumps into catastrophes /
last looks into the molten core of the world /
demanding brevity / a ruthless red penciller
of romantic flights of fancy and gushing streams
of exuberance / this is why i'm a poet / a chronicler
of the essence of things / a syllabic counter of the
most brutal sort / where all roads come to a
denouement without doubt or curfew or apology /
gurgling out across the tilled tundra of the earth /
without rolling up its sleeves or beating down doors
with a heavy wind / short / to the core / the nitty
gritty / brevis interuptus / of remarkable things
my grandpa explained to me in the dark

i have recently joined a new religion. this religion shortens everything. i.e. danielle becomes dani. our leader believes everything is overdone and overlong. by chopping down things to manageable size we live with less. for example, this afternoon instead of jogging three miles i jogged around the block. i've taken to buying expensive hardcover editions of new biographies of labor leaders of the 1930s but only read the first chapter. i only go to see the first ten minutes of movies. i only sleep three hours a night. i only eat two meals a day. i only wear one sock. i shower every other day. i only shampoo half my hair and shave half of my face. this is a liberating experience. try driving or walking halfway to work. try shoveling half the snow on the sidewalk. try frying half a chicken. try getting half the flu. try living on half your salary. read half the bible. meditate on being half empty. fill the other half with a pound of rich hazelnut chocolate from belgium. learn the symbolism of half the paintings of heronimous bosch. become a partial surrealist. memorize the first verse of america the beautiful. recycle half of every six-pack. laugh out of one corner of your mouth.

your pal,

bo

There Are Too Many Words In My House

For Dayl

there are too many words in my house. they came in through the bathroom window last summer and they've multiplied a thousand fold. they've entered books and spawned like psychopaths. turning every surface into encyclopedias. threatening me with their perspicacity. their loquaciousness. their arrogance. sticking their tongue out when i'm watching some stupid sitcom on tv or laughing hysterically over my adolescent behavior when i scream at my wife for making me drippy oatmeal for breakfast. the only time i'm at peace is when the words adopt the role of poets. sitting there contemplating the quiet in the woods beside the house. or riding on a big wave of inspiration about the transformation of night into day. or the amazing awakening of things right outside our front door. sometimes the cats come out from underneath the couch or from behind the washing machine and tangle gently with the words. coaxing them to coo or whistle or make funny sounds like a caboose on a train in a children's picture book when you're five. i'm planning on taking a cue from the cats. softly persuading the words to take a sunday stroll down the road. to stretch their syllables out for a brief spell. and then quickly closing the window behind them so they're gone. so i'm free of an overdose of words. filling every available space so there's nearly no room for air. and if i miss the words too much i'll make an appointment with them for tea and they'll come dressed in their sunday best and we'll talk about the new vocabulary they've learned this week and then bid adieu like ex-housemates till we meet up again someday in the great library in the sky.

There's a Z Crossing the Sky

there's a z crossing the sky. creating more excitement than independence day. it's a bolt of lightning charging the sky with ions. it's a baby zebra galloping across a field of night. it's the closing remark of zorro wielding his signature with his sword before jettisoning into disappearance. this z is breathing like an accordion. its skin pliable as plastic. capable of creating a high c or tumbling into the depths of b minor. a beam of electric light zooms out from its forehead. illuminating the road home. crowded with pilgrims and mendicants asking for a sign of god's love. z's gather in the sky like a child's toy train. hooting and whistling and rumbling. announcing its next destination. when we get on board we dream about zoos and zylophones and our friend zack and z's leap from the train's smokestack and everyone runs out of their houses and tumblesaults figure-8's and follows the train of z's for miles and miles and miles and we go home and wait for the z's return and cross our fingers and get down on our knees and look up at the stars and suddenly z's twitter like a school of robins and fill the sky with laughter.

True Love

It was an intricate, intimate moment in time.
It was a path that was traveled by true wayfarers.
It was the highest compliment paid to the worthless and nameless.
I shook off its epiphanies like a flea.
I traveled its roads like a private Buddha.
I took its pulse with a tourniquet wrapped around the muscles of its heart.
I splashed blood from my open wounds across its dazzling panorama.
I laughed aloud and stared the doubters down.
Was I losing my mind or was my faith being twisted into an impossible puzzle?
More difficult to solve than a Rubik's Cube?
More difficult than Borges' Labyrinth?
More difficult than Newton's Laws of Probability.
When the insurmountable was surmounted,
I cried a Caspian Sea of tears.
I yawned and the whole world spilled from my mouth,
I sat down and memorized everything worth remembering.
Then I called you on the phone and apologized for loving you too much.

[Jonathan Rose and Bruce Weber]

where are the ants running to? under the beams of the house? within the electrical wiring? into the internal secrets of the plumbing? are they in quest of the house's secret hiding place? where mice, insects and bees gather for communal dinners under the nose of the burghers who think their lives are in perfectly respectable order? poets debate such things. splitting hairs across the marvelous terrain of the universe. gears sputtering. the sun spreading its warmth like butter on freshly baked bread. philosophizing about the secrets laying under the surface of everything. the disgust gathering for years under the thick shag carpet / the dust of the withered rose shattering like so many pieces of crushed glass under the ballerina's slippers / the booming of shotguns in the distance snagging a gaggle of geese. sit. be patient. watch the ants collecting crumbs. measuring up the moral dilemna of us all. carrying off the small infinitesimal things we shake off our shoulders like water splattering everywhere.

The Woods Beside The House

For Joanne

she saw a lot of strange birds this morning. one flew in circles around the hibiscus flower. one managed to swallow an early apple from the branch of the old orchard tree. one gathered worms before lifting into the sky like a helicopter. these strange beautiful creatures tantalized her imagination. made her swing through the air like a cowboy's lasso. exchanged her vocabulary of rocks and snails and paper dolls for aeronautic words like wind thrust or avalanche till she was turned inside out with confusion about wind and the islands of sanctuary in her rear view mirror and the path through the tall cedar grove lined with stones awaiting the accidental slip of a shoe. the birds lifted her out of the ordinary. planted her on tinsel-covered earth. juggled her sense of propriety like the samba. till the forest was dancing with a fortitude everyone's mother's would be proud of. and there on a branch — just out of sniffing range of the mischievous cat — was a potpourri of birds creating a morning parade of colors and wondrous whistles sure to entice even the most lopsided out of tune ear into a symphonic celebration of the woods beside the house.

Max's White Rope

Max has this rope
It's a white rope
It's long as a rattle snake
It curls and glides
Along the cherry wood floor
Whispering something in Max's ear
Is there some strange ghost living in the rope?
Is there some miracle hibernating in the throat of the rope?
Is there some amazing chirp making a home in the heart of the rope?
What impels Max to pull this rope
Across the length and breadth of this house
Like it's some kind of key to a golden door
Max wants to open more than anything?
Maybe it's simpler than a big dream
Maybe it's quite practical
Maybe Max just likes to jump after the rope
Max likes to scheme after the rope
Max likes to entangle himself like a silly boy in the rope
Crossing the threshold of each day
With a pursuit as pure as an uncut diamond
And coming along behind him always
The white rope
The white rope curled like a serpent
The white rope tugged across exotic continents
Max's rope
Max's white rope

An Enigma

an enigma. mark said. it was something that slipped between the fingers. that loosed itself on the world like a five hundred mile an hour tornado. cutting down forests. knocking over unsteady buildings. wrestling the heads off wild dogs. adjusting the margins of the world so there were no loose edges. no inadvertent elbows. no steps across the boundaries of the day like an unruly family of frogs. it was an enigma that troubled mark. that made him toss and turn like a slithery snake following the path of least resistance to chomp on the poor child's gangly leg. that transported him through the world like a shaky pen in an old man's hand. that proscribed him to a lean life of sarcasm and irritability unless he unlocked the key of enigma. the shadowy interior of enigma. the fuzzy implications of enigma. so mark chiseled and chiseled and chiseled till the enigma gave way to a perfectly clear afternoon. till the temperature was around sixty. till everything was as explainable as the abc's to a properly functioning toddler. and mark would laugh reading italo calvino. imagining every speck in the cosmos. taking his mind on a long ride across the meanings and shadows of things. sticking enigma in his back pack. taking it along on the train ride to sarajevo / to beirut / to the desert kingdom of sudan.

She Overlooked Everything

She overlooked everything.
That was her protocol.
The sun set.
The moon rose.
She overlooked everything.
The cat meowed.
The dog barked.
She overlooked everything.
When I was ten I told her I loved her.
I swore on her heart like the full moon.
I swayed like a ship in the thralls of a storm.
I promised her riches and children and thunder.
That was before the balloon fell.
Before the canyons flooded.
Before the story got out to the press.
Nowadays we sweat like hogs and mow the lawn.
We tumble like bear cubs and throw salt.
The victorious girls of the neighboring woods.
The yellow flag raised as high as the steeple of the church.
The crucifix bleeding miracles in the basement down the road.
She overlooked everything.
A puzzle of mumbles.
A pickering of thumbs.
The imminent decay of a shoulderless day.

She Should Be With The Other Dolls

she should be with the other dolls
but
they
pull
her
hair,
they
rip
her
dress,
they
play
havoc
with
her sleep,
her dreams,
her yearnings,
tugging at her long eyelashes,
poking
her
with
spiders,
scissoring up her undergarments.
she should be with the other dolls
but
they
gossip
about
her reputation,
her
sexual
persuasion,
her
passion,
like a trail of fire's running across her skin,
branding every soul she touches.
she should be with the other dolls
but they say
she's
got

a
pact
with
satan,
they
say
she's
manipulated
the
little
girl
to
love
her
best,
to
cling
to
her
at
the
ring
of nightfall,
to hold her
through
every
shadowy
dream,
so they shush her away,
they push her off the shelf,
fling
her
onto
the
floor,
so
she
tumbles,
smashing
her
plastic
bottom.

Eleven Things I Have To Do

1. Return the hand grenade that Marty's father gave me after the war.
2. Clean out the shed of all lingering memories.
3. Opine for Ophelia.
4. Hiccup quietly.
5. Bring home as many rocks as possible from the old mine.
6. Ask Marvin for a loan till Independence Day.
7. Apologize to Mary for breaking the bell candle.
8. Hand Tommy a banjo and ask him to play *Oh Susanna*.
9. Grin so wide the stars align with the earth.
10. Clear the pile of rubble from the road with dispatch.
11. Walk in taller shoes.

Between the Wars

you remind me
of the years between the wars
when love surrendered easily
and time fluttered its wings
like a bat out of hell,
it was then that you came to me
carrying on
about the weight of his refusals
about the glimmer in his eye
about the terrain of his tempestuouness
leaning on the table
with a heavy fist
and dreams broken
like eggs
on the hotplate of the sidewalk,
staring into some blank abyss
where the clocks hands
turn unmercifully
in endless circles
and women curtsy
and men pin carnations on their lapel
and the sun sets in the morning
and nighttime is alive with colored shadows
that recline in the tubes of the painters
and geneva purrs on with business
and a glass raised to neutrality,
and the skeleton bones
of the helpless dead
slip under the white sheets
of the morgue
and the windows open
and the bodies jump
and the streets are scarred
with the war dead,
and you stretch your hand out
shaking off kindness like a leaf
slinging apologies like soft bullets

reminding us of time's follies
and the wicked playthings
with their jagged elbows,
love breaking mirrors
love climbing to the roof
love storming the barricades
love sleeping in the park
love joining the folds
of life together
like busy ants
running
into
the
pyre
of
the
day

When Bob Left

When Bob left
I wet myself
Like a baby boy.
I lassoed hope
And threw it
Into the East River.
I watched time collapse
Into a big fat zero.

When Bob left
I broke a wrist.
I lost my job.
I was investigated by the IRS.

When Bob left
The children sniffled.
The police siren whistled.
The clouds drifted across the sky like flag covered coffins.

When Bob left
The universe went babaloo.
The answer to all my questions disappeared into the ether.
I was left alone at the side of the road
Watching life pass by without a single chuckle.

When Bob left
I apologized for all the wrongs I ever did.
I galloped away at the speed of light.
I composed a one hundred and twenty eight and a half minute requiem.

When Bob left
I pursued the angel of death with a raised shoe.
I demanded an apology from the CEO living in the penthouse.
I descended on the scene of the crime with a stare that could freeze a dragon.

When Bob left
I crawled on a hundred chards of broken glass.
I stumbled into a downpour of rain.
I ponied up to G-d for a fucking reason.

CONVALESCENCE

It's talkative as a broken tape-recorder. Essential as a fresh breath of air inside a vacuum. It's incapable of being condensed or abridged or red-penciled to oblivion. Something thrown together in a knitting circle. Roped together by a happy-go-lucky cowboy. Ricocheted off the walls of a handball court. It's the sum of all things. The reverberation inside a piano. It's touchy-feely. Green as Courbert's ocean or Whistler's Thames. Take it up your nose and sniff it. Inhale its aroma deep in your mind like hope or faith or charity. Cling to it in winter. In the dark uncertainty of its fall from grace. Its pas de deux with love beauty death and decay. Hold it tightly. Never let it stroll farther than an infant's first steps. Draw it into the folds of your existence like water wind and the wobbly path we walk down to Judgment Day among boulders bees barking dogs and the twinkling of faraway stars.

She Understood the Temperament Of Rain

she understood the temperament of rain.
wore galoushes on dry sunny days.
prepared for any sudden shifts in the weather.

an intermittent cry for help.
the gulping.
the swallowing.
the urge to vanish
like raindrops down the drain.

she measured out droplets from a syringe.
counted up how much it required
for her to escape pain for another day.
her pockets turned inside out.
her face narrow as a house of falling cards.

sometimes she'd reach for a cloud in her dreams.
grabbing it out of the thick air like a truant officer.
the long walk off the cliff.
the water cascading.
the body swallowed up.
the rain hard as nails.
closing the coffin lid.

the rain.
the endless rain.
the endless endless rain.

The Trouble With Annie

The black-eyed boy.
The canary-yellow shoes.
The unlucky red car.
These things trouble Annie.
Tie a bow around her finger.
Demand unction at Sunday mass.
Tussle with the resolute spirit's of priests.
The rushing waters.
The choking closet.
The reprehensible couch.
These disasters spin endless wheels.
Amuse themselves among the raindrops.
Convince Annie to blow herself up like a balloon.
Floating beyond irreducible odds / inconsequential pleas.
The irreverent crow.
The irascible squirrel.
The snippety merchant of dreams.
These creatures congratulate Annie
For
Her preposterous green eyes
Her welcoming remarks to honey bees.
Her wider-than-the-night-sky-smile.

eddie walked into the wall and said to the wall hello how are you wall and eddie galloped all the way to school just in case the teacher decided to read his favorite story about the pony and the boy who rode upon its back everywhere. and eddie sentenced his imagination to a lengthy sojurn on the ship cleopatra sailing down the nile sipping from a straw and smiling all the way to the land of ra. and eddie gulped and gulped and gulped again in anticipation of restoring his powers of creation. simmering like a pot on the half boil in quest of becoming clear purified water. and eddie leaped and spit and sizzled and jumped through the hoop of the moon alarming the mice under the kitchen sink. scaring away the creepy spiders aching to hypnotize him into coming close enough to be bitten. waving bye bye to bats flying around the attic. and eddie jumped and guffawed and walked and sailed and hypnotized and galavanted and simmered and waved so long to all the draggy things that used to make him mud waddle and now put a smile across the panorama of his face as enigmatic as the mona lisa. and eddie laughs and cries and spins and giggles in the face of evil frightening evil away one two three.

Convalescence

when i was growing up my fingers throbbed from turning so many pages. the weight of *a tale of two cities* almost crushed me. the nurses were pleasant. the doctors made me promise to embrace sleep as an ally but i read under the cover of night with my flashlight devouring *the arabian nights* and *tales of the brothers grimm*. i danced around the truth till the truth waltzed away shyly. defending myself from the sheepish questions of lovers by reading till dawn crept under the door quiet as a lamb. the convalescence was sweet. a victory for my fingers and my soul. i charted the wonders of every page like a merchant adding up sous while butterflies sprinted across the garden like mcabees. playing tag with sparrows. pole vaulting petunias and bee alms. anticipating the whir of the engine and the tumult of turning gears chomping on grass. the butterflies disappeared after that summer. a pall was cast over their beauty that stung. the endless days of pouring rain drowned everything. even emily dickinson's poems couldn't keep the butterflies in tow. the falling of summer on their delicate skin, breaking the thread of their conversation with the sun. a sudden thud on the roof of all that happened that summer while my fingers silently healed.

The Starlight Of Heaven

She is so terrified.
The last time
She sank so deep
The sky started falling.
And when the flock of seagulls
Flew by
She was trembling
So bad
The wind
Felt like a crutch
She could stand on.
"The better to eat you with"
Said the constant reminder
In her imagination
About love and war
And hunting out of season.
Someday she'll recover
And be on time
For her graduation
From the School of Freud
Into the Starlight of Heaven.

A Poem In Forty Five Parts

1.
strange murmurings among the amaryllis.

2.
it was half past seven.
the cats meowed at the moon.

3.
stop.
look around.
wink at god.
proceed with care.

4.
follow your instincts to the river.
discover her body among the willow trees.

5.
sometimes a few words can change everything.

6.
sometimes fingerprints blur.

7.
after the funeral she flew to guadalajara.

8.
after the investigation everyone slept like the baby jesus.

9.
her tears flooded the old house of creeky hinges.

10.
a few laughs.
a few beers.

11.
the anthropologist said there would be eras exactly like this.

12.
in point of fact
everything
was
a
mirage.

illusory.
foggy.
impossible
to
coerce
into
a legible score
or
a
hummable melody.

13.
she could not explain why he slipped out of her hands.

14.
afternoons sometimes flew by like witch's on broomsticks.

15.
there is nothing left, she said.

16.
flap your wings like an eagle, he said.

17.
the crinkling of bags made him angry as a nosediving pilot.

18.
quiet is a fragile thing.
pressing his ear to the pond.

19.
spit far
er.

20.
the alarm sounded.
he was caught with his pants down.
the newspapers ate it up.
bail was set at 6 million.
his face scowled up
like a pussy cat
accidentally
jumping
into
a
vat
of
sulphuric
acid.

21.
after the river was cleaned up.
the company's profits rose seven hundred percent.

22.
a can of beans.

23.
the gun barely went off.
but she was dead.

24.
the memorial service was a wholesome affair.
it was televised.
the nation was pleased by all this.

25.
sometimes the plainest things are unwashable.

26.
he pledged allegiance to his country.
the room shook like point 7 on the richter scale.

27.
haiku's make him scratch his head.

28.
he remembered sleeping under the pool table in the london waif's home.

29.
he recalled desert nights and a long tongue kiss from a chicago girl named loey.

30.
a blank wall.

31.
she rose a fist into the sky
before depositing a round of bullets in her throat.

32.
following the third funeral in days he moved away.

33.
sometimes he even denied he ever lived there.

34.
days passed into decades.

35.
the anxiety was enough to burn down the house.

36.
she slapped herself and looked around to see if anyone noticed.

37.
the sun dropped below the horizon like a sleepy hound dog.

38.
he was feeling chilly.

39.
the clouds drifted across the sky with a thump.

40.
he needed a stiff drink and a visit to the red light district.

41.
the full moon made him blush.

42.
it was approaching midnight.

43.
the black cat swam across the thames.

44.
the pounding bells of big ben.

45.
he was glad to be alive.

Impressions of Machu Pichu

1.

breathless. a breathless experience.
beyond clouds. sea. earth. here
the sun & the moon dance together.
here the stars align with the gods
& the heavens open like spring
flowers. here the mysteries of the
universe propel things infinitesimally
along in a cosmic spiral. across
galaxies. in the grasp of unfathomable
things. the entrance gate. the temple
of the sun. the tower. the stone quarry.
the amphitheatre. the meditation room.
the condors. the orchids. the thatched
roofs. the distance between things.
the narrow distance between things.
crowding ourselves between stone
& chisel. hammer & nail. breath
& unbreath. out of reach of the stars.

2.

this town wakes at noon. the condor's
throw sleep off their shoulders and
swoop into town square stalking
children & enticing young girls
to hurl pieces of chicken and lamb.
the goats come too. bringing fortune
and rusty tin cans. entertaining the
crowds with their jangly music.
somtimes i sit cross legged by the
fountain playing flute. mimicking
the whoosh of the condor's wings
as they circle above awaiting prey.
my music dangles from the ears
of women like silver rings nestled

in amaranth or takes flight among
the industrious ants carrying crumbs
to their lair out of the sight of the
town. i play till stars appear in the
sky & the northern one becomes as
big as a flying saucer leaving behind
a trail of wonder. this is typical of my
day. counting the soles slung in my pail.
their richochet heard as far as machu
pichu some kilometers up the road
mingled between the mist & stars.

If I Could Paint I'd Consider the Canvas a Door

if i could paint i'd consider the canvas a door. the image would be completely flat. color would be subtle. light browns and yellows. the door's handle would be broken. a screwdriver would hang from a cord. when i grab for the door handle it would fall and shatter. if i pressed my eye to the keyhole i would be surprised to discover an orchestra. the conductor is not marcel duchamp but piranesi, the italian obsessed with ruins. piranesi is asking the third violin to play with feeling on the third movement when the shopkeeper discovers his sister has been beaten by the 3rd grade teacher. at this point i pull my eye from the keyhole and eliminate the screwdriver, the teacher, piranesi and the orchestra. what remains is a door.

Blue Poem #2

Contagious blue.
Sic em on me blue.
Humming bird blue.
Yes
Talk to me blue.
Whistle a happy tune blue.
Greet me with a smile as broad
As Gainsborough's Little Boy Blue.
An incident in blue
Perculating in the memory of an old man
Remembering the freedom of his youth
Sailing on the tip of his tongue
In quest of a woman
To heal all his blue encumbrances.
A blue day leapfrogging gray days
In the mine fields of the imagination
Or skateboarding across the lush terrain of Ireland
On a perfectly blue summer afternoon.
A juggernaut of blue.
A bombastic terrain of blue.
A kimosabie blue.
Eating
Blue plums
Blue fish
Blue berries
In a world completely under the thrall of
Ethereal blue
Taking my breath away blue
Following you to the ends of the earth blue.

the air whistles through the street in search of charley parker's perfect harmonies.
the bright sun sets on the crowded boulevard.
the lamp post sings the blues in rhythm with the clouds and faraway stars.
the rustling of fish taking a swim.
the turning wheels of the old steam boat.
the ferryman waving his weary arms.
someday things will be different for you and i.
the running of a small child's feet.
the porridge spooned into a hungry mouth.
i will love you with a faith that never grows cold.
tacking the sail before quietly moving on.

You #1

You are the joy at the end of the rainbow.
The sniff of something callifragilistic
At the crossroads of love and hate.
The pure reason
That feeds the dark heart of the engine
On impossible missions
To recover beauty for beauty's sake.
You are the tumult
In the washing machine's engine
Spewing madness
Among the blossoming cherry blossoms.
The remembrance of a golden walk
In springtime along the banks of the River Zu.
You are the passion
Spilling out like a ripe coconut.
The congealing that lingers
Between star-crossed lovers
In that film down at the mall.
The promise that flies in the face of the sun.
The serpent that leaps into the unknown.
The parabola that breaks down enroute to Brooklyn.
The hair raising antics of a juggler
Hell bent on throwing a dozen
Switchblades in the air.
The optimum temperature of survival.
The broken dish mended by a wish and a prayer.
You are all that and so much more.
I can't deal with it.
Much less define it.
Explicate it.
Reason with it.
Break it down into phonemes.
You rock.
You fern.
You tree.
You lip.
You frog.

You toy.
You tot.
You imp.
You submarine.
You aircraft carrier.
You intimate whisper.
You long lasting kiss.
You implication that left the room.
You left turn at the light.
You rumination that spins
Around in endless swirls
Before ascending
To your great heights.
Your towering stories.
Your great plains.
Your warm bed
At the end of a very long day.

you're a handshake from god. a long tongue kiss in the dark. a 3, 4, 5, 6 in a game of pick up stix. you're like a drug i want to confide in. you're like a dog i want to play with. you're like a whisper i want to press my ear close to. you're like an assumption without any scientific proof required. you're magnetic at both ends. resourceful as two twigs rubbed together causing fire. you're cuter than that angel in the painting by botticelli. you're more remarkable than that clairvoyant preaching on his street corner soapbox. you're friendlier than that spider frightening little billy. you're capable of flinging the weight of the world off your shoulders and not feeling responsible for the resulting topspin. you glow in the dark like a visitor from another planet. you flock like a school of robins toward the window waving bye bye. you leap like a doe over my lumpy existence. you're memories of florence on a golden afternoon conversing with massacio and the carmelites. you're onions that don't burn my eyes. you're answers to unfathomable questions. you're gongs going off in my head come new year's. without you i'm flustered. i'm cold gravy. i'm goo goo gaa gaa. i'm quixotic. i'm xenophobic. i'm catatonic. i'm toasted. i'm clutching the monkey. i'm lip-synching the chorus to hair. i'm divining that angel at the fire and dime with my lightening rod. i'm crumbling like all those public schools in brooklyn. i'm zeroing in on your tuba. i'm playing scales along your rib-cage. i'm thirstier than a desert. i'm pushing up daisies.

Interiors - Paintings by Arturo Rodriguez

Interior 1

Interior 4

Interior 7

Interior 12

INTERIORS

1

a
house
perched
on the edge of the imagination
somewhere ghostly thin
occupied by colored air
and
television light
ethereal
fog-like spectres
of a world
interrupted by airplanes
and running children
caught
in
a
tailwind of electricity
and
thunder
of
interrogations
in
clandestine rooms
below
the
earth's
skin
closed
to
light
and
wind
and
the
endless
shifting
of
clouds

he remembers
the overflowing river
his brother swimming away
his father standing tall
on the edge of the house
the walls cracking
the daylight seeping in
surrending to so much water
in this dream
he swims
endlessly
homeless
rudderless
anchorless
withour mooring
imagines breathing in the river
inhaling every current into his skin
the house floating away
the house floating downriver
the house surrendering to the pull of the day

3

he comes out of the closet and joins me for a drink. we clink glasses and recall perfectly sunny days in cuba. the wind blowing softly through the tobacco fields. my father raising a toast to life's simple pleasures. and he slaps me on the back and coaxes me to drink till my words slur and i am lost to the world and my eyes close and I sleep. and he opens drawyers. he helps himself to dinner. he lingers before my canvas changing values. rearranging cast shadows. and i sleep. i sleep.

4

sometimes he climbs the walls at night when I am sleeping. opening closets. removing photographs from envelopes. reading my mail. he arrived when I was a child. following my mother in when she was returning from the hospital. when i paint he is with me. standing beside my canvas. watching. like a mirror of my darkest inclinations. the ones that shooed me under the bed as a child. the ones that wrestled with my uncle when he lost control of his imagination. sometimes at night i study the silhouettes of shadows. raising a toast to all the things i do not understand. sometimes i toss rocks down an endless gulley. listening to their richochets. in my paintings I keep these incidents in balance. brown plays against yellow. gray plays against blue. passages of white are cool. areas of relief and meditation. like clouds. white passing clouds. and i am moving across the sky like a ship in the night. its sails high. pressed along by wind. a strong wind. throwing everything into relief. in this labyrinthe i sit drinking another glass of wine. forgetting the shadows lingering just out of reach of my brush.

5

draw the curtain
the scene
a basement
gray
green
hints of blue
a girl asleep in the corner
a man on a ladder tipping
a woman on the bottom step
balanced
like
a
dancer
the light streaming in
soft caressing
a chair alone
empty
beside the tall ladder
awaiting
a
guest
a glass of wine
a kiss in the dark
an episode of love
the man on the ladder
caught in the forgiving hands of the woman
balancing herself on air
like a magician
tipping into
d
a
y
l
i
g
h
t

6

there is an unequilibrium here
everything falling
slipping
trying to catch its breath
the furniture shifts places
and ghosts amuse themselves
with my fragile samovar
the shape of the rooms change
like mercury or quicksilver
windows disappear
under this spell
of
unbalance
tipping closed
far from my outstretched arms
the interior of this house
a
cave
a
deep
cavity
inside
the
earth
past
present
future
all alike
all alluring
protecting me from strong winds
threatening me with strong winds
someday I will discover
the open door
and
right behind it
the blue sky
welcoming me in its arms

7

there is no certainty here
everything mist
diahonous
toxic
the road full of boulders and dragons of the imagination
people walking walking walking
homeless
bereft
of
shelter
security
splattered
like
blood
on
the
walls
on
the
floor
on
the
furniture
only the telephone poles will remain someday
scattered across the globe
like dinosaur skeletons
poems will be bartered for apples
and
paintings will be exchanged for clean water
certainty will end here
among
the
fishes
swallowing
for
air

among
the
children
turning
the
endless
wheel
of
the
bicycle
among
the
strangers
picking
up
spades
to
bury
the
dead
the air moist
thick with fog
covering the earth
with
mournfulness
the
steps
one
after
another
steps
one
after
another
steps
one
after
another

8

sometimes you come looking for me
and i'm climbing a ladder
to the stars
you laugh
and throw pennies at the moon
i catch them with my teeth
like i'm biting into a long stemmed rose
you think this is funny
and wave your red cloak
at me
like a bull
ready to extinguish
its anger
our imaginary child
sleeps in the basement
our imaginary daughter
asleep in the corner of the room
underneath us
drifting in
with the tide
departing with each
call of the moon

i sit in this chair
and watch the world
tumble
to the ground
it's safe here
among
familiar
things
the neighbor practicing balance in the yard
tiptoeing through the air
in search of rapture and release
the walkers on the beach
holding parasols above their head
dodging the traffic of the waves
and the harsh memories of yesterday's storm
when the air cut through the town
lancing houses, schools, office towers
and i could barely breath
in & out
in & out
till balance was restored
and I could rest on the balls of my feet
stepping forward
like an old friend
capable of sharing
laughter
or
a
drink
in the hard rain
of
expectations
the doors open to the tide
the man drifts by on a floating roof
the walls shift their weight
against
the

roar
of
a
wave
but I sit here
gathering dreams
in
a restful world
prepared for any pratfall
or sudden slipping
into the shiftng tide
removing
uncertainty
from
its
tug
on
my
collar
safe
in the warmth
of
a
familiar
chair
and
the
certainty
of
four
strong
walls

APPENDIX

Alphabetical Index Of Poems

#

A

B

C

D

E

Alphabetical Index Of Poems

•

ROGUE SCHOLARS
Press

For General Information, go to:

http://www.roguescholars.com

For more information or a price quote for our
book design and editing services, contact:

editor@roguescholars.com

•

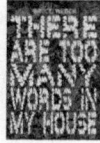

There Are Too Many Words In My House
Bruce Weber
13: 978-1-942463-03-0

Driving The Celexa
Miriam Stanley
978-0-9840982-7-9

A Poem Of Common Prayer
Larry Jones
978-0-9840982-2-4

Let's Fly To Trazodone
Miriam Stanley
978-0-9840982-6-2

The Breakup Of My First Marriage
Bruce Weber
978-0-9771550-9-5

Get Over It!
Miriam Stanley
978-0-9771550-6-4

Expectations
Gary Beck
978-0-9840982-0-0

Out Of And Into The Fray
Eugene Ring
978-0-9840982-1-7

Not To Be Believed
Miriam Stanley
978-0-9771550-3-3

Lazarus
Jean Lehrman
978-0-9771550-5-7

For Better Or Verse
Tom Guarnera
978-0-9771550-4-0

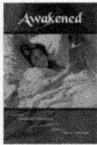

Awakened
Madeline Artenberg / Iris N. Schwartz
978-0-9771550-1-9

Anthologies:

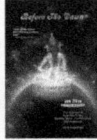

Before The Dawn - 2019
An ANYDSWPE Anthology
978-0-9840982-8-6

Pa'lante A La Luz (Charge Into The Light) - 2018
An ANYDSWPE Anthology
978-0-9840982-5-5

Forever Night (Siempre Noche) - 2017
An ANYDSWPE Anthology
978-0-9840982-4-8

Palabras Luminosas (Luminous Words) - 2016
An ANYDSWPE Anthology
978-0-9840982-3-1

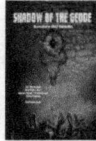

Shadow Of The Geode (Sombra Del Geode) - 2015
An ANYDSWPE Anthology
978-1-942463-00-9 [Bonsai Publishers, 1st Edition]

Estrellas En El Fuego (Stars In The Fire) - 2014
An ANYDSWPE Anthology
978-0-9840982-9-3

Cat Breath
A Two-Headed Kitty Anthology
978-0-9771550-2-6

In The Company Of Rogues
Out Of Print

0.0 (Zero Point Zero)
Out of Print

www.ingramcontent.com/pod-product-compliance
Lightning Source LLC
Chambersburg PA
CBHW021201020426
42331CB00003B/165